Hilary Koll and Steve Mills

S0-BMT-702

Contents

Introduction

Children between the ages of 7 and 11 (Years 3–6) study Key Stage 2 of the National Curriculum. In May of their final year in Key Stage 2 (Year 6) all children take written National Tests (commonly known as SATs) in English, Mathematics and Science. The tests are carried out in school, under the supervision of teachers, but are marked by examiners outside the school.

Pupils also have their school work assessed by their teachers. These assessments will be set alongside your child's results in the National Tests. In July these results will be reported to you, enabling you and your child's teacher to see whether your child is reaching national standards set out in the National Curriculum. The report will highlight your child's strengths and achievements and will suggest targets for development. Each child will probably spend about five hours in total sitting the tests during one week in May. Most children will do two papers in Science and three papers in Mathematics and English.

Understanding your child's level of achievement

The National Curriculum divides standards of performance in each subject into a number of levels, from 1 to 8. On average, children are expected to advance one level for every two years they are at school. By the end of Key Stage 2 (Year 6), your child should be at Level 4.

If your child is working at Level 3, there will be some areas of Maths that they will need help with. If your child is working at Level 5 or above, they are doing very well, and are exceeding the targets for their age group.

The table shows how your child should progress through the levels at ages 7, 11 and 14 (the end of Key Stages 1, 2 and 3).

	7 years	11 years	14 years
level 8+			☐
level 8			■
level 7			■
level 6		☐	☐
level 5		■	☐
level 4	☐	☐	▨
level 3	■	▨	▨
level 2	☐	▨	▨
level 1	▨	▨	▨

☐ Exceptional performance
■ Exceeded targets for age group
☐ Achieved targets for age group
▨ Working towards targets for age group

The Tests in Mathematics

The National Curriculum divides Mathematics at Key Stage 2 into four areas or Attainment Targets. These are 'Using and Applying Mathematics', which is assessed through classroom work, and 'Number', 'Shape, Space and Measure' and 'Data Handling', for which there are written tests.

Mental Mathematics Test

This short test contains questions that are orally delivered (through a cassette tape) and require children to answer mentally in 5, 10 or 15 seconds. This test makes up 20% of your child's overall mark.

Written Mathematics Tests A and B (Both 45 minutes)
Levels 3–5

These tests contain Number, Shape, Space and Measure and Data Handling questions. The questions are a mixture of Levels 3–5 work and children are expected to attempt as many questions as they can. At present, Test A is a non-calculator test and Test B is a calculator test. Test B, therefore, contains more complex problems to solve, whilst Test A has a greater proportion of quick calculations.

Extension to Level 6 (40 minutes)

This test can be taken by children who are thought to be achieving Level 5 with confidence. It contains work studied at Key Stage 3 and is achieved by children who are working at a level of mathematics beyond their years.

Tests are sent away by the school to be externally marked. The marks for Tests A and B and the Mental Test are combined and the total mark will indicate a level. These will be N, 2, 3, 4, or 5. N indicates when a child did not score sufficient points to obtain a Level 2 or higher. Children taking the extension paper may obtain a Level 6 or not. If Level 6 is not reached, the Level obtained in the other tests stands.

The expected level in the Key Stage 2 National Tests is Level 4.

There are three self-tests in this book to reflect the three Attainment Target areas tested in the Key Stage 2 National Tests, that is, Number, Shape, Space and Measure, and Data Handling. Some extension material is provided in this book for children working at Level 5, including work on Algebra, Imperial measurements, Angle and Pie charts.

How this book will help

- This book provides the essential knowledge needed by your child to tackle the Mathematics Tests with confidence.
- It revises work your child should be doing in class. It does not attempt to teach new material from scratch.
- This book is designed to help your child prepare for the tests. It includes activities to help your child improve understanding of the topics through extended practice carried out independently.
- Useful 'tips' help your child to develop their work.
- Tests (Test yourself pages) allow your child informal practice in answering the kinds of questions asked in the National Tests.
- Answers are provided on pages 46–48 to enable your child to learn from mistakes.

Using this book

Short questions can be answered on the page, but have some spare paper available for your child to use when working on the activities. In encouraging your child, remember the 'little and often' rule. Make sure the atmosphere is relaxed when this book is used. It can be returned to it again and again, but try to make sure your child does not spend too much time worrying, and encourage a relaxed and confident approach. Help your child to see the SATs tests as an opportunity to demonstrate knowledge rather than worrying about any difficulties. This book has been designed to provide a fun way of practising the skills and revising knowledge necessary for your child to produce the best possible work in the National Tests.

Solving number problems (1)

Number problems can be worked out **in your head** or **on paper.** Look out for these words:

Addition:	plus	add	altogether
	total	increase by	more
	sum		
Subtraction:	take away	less	subtract
	difference	minus	fewer
	discount	decrease by	
Multiplication:	multiply	product	multiplied by
	groups of	times	
Division:	divide	divided by	share
	remainder		

Calculating in your head

33 + 19

- When adding 10, just add 1 to the tens column.

  $$482 + 10 = 492$$

- When subtracting 10, just subtract 1 ten from the tens column.

  $$482 - 10 = 472$$

- When multiplying by 10 move each digit across one place to the left.

  $$482 \times 10 = 4820$$

- When dividing by 10 move each digit across one place to the right.

Th	H	T	U.	t
	4	8	2.	
		4	8.	2

÷ 10 $482 \div 10 = 48.2$

Solving number problems (2)

Calculating on paper

Adding and subtracting

Line the columns up, units under units and tens under tens, etc.

Watch out for when you need to exchange.

$676 + 287$ $1521 - 784$

```
   H T U
   6 7 6
 + 2 8 7
 ───────
   9 6 3
   1 1
```

```
 Th H  T  U
  1  14 11/12  11
 ─  7  8  4
 ──────────
    7  3  7
```

Multiplying and dividing

Here are some ways of doing multiplication and division.

576×8 26×12 $375 \div 6$

```
 Th H T U
    5 7 6
 ×      8
 ────────
  4 6 0 8
    6   4
```

```
   H T U
     2 6
 ×   1 2
 ───────
   2 6 0
     5 2
 ───────
   3 1 2
     1
```

```
    0 6 2 r3
 6 ) 3 7¹5

 Answer = 62 r3
```

If you do it in a different way, that's fine, as long as you get the right answer!

Question

Work these out on a piece of paper:

$581 + 346$
$2351 - 672$
542×5
23×24
$51 \div 3$
$200 \div 25$

Tip

If you know the answer to one multiplication question you can find others easily. If you know that
$24 \times 173 = 4152$, then
$2\mathbf{5} \times 173$ is 173 more than 4152
and
$24 \times 17\mathbf{4}$ is 24 more than 4152.

3 Solving number problems (3)

Money and measurements

When adding, subtracting, multiplying or dividing ...

... watch out for

- **pounds** and **pence.** Change the numbers so that they are all pounds, or all pence: £1.26 or 126p.

- **metres** and **centimetres.** Change the numbers so that they are all metres, or all centimetres: 1.86 m or 186 cm

Look at this example:

> Amy has £1. She buys some sweets and is given 42p change. How much did she spend on sweets?

This is a subtraction question. Change to pence or pounds:

100p − ? = 42p   **or**   £1 − ? = £0.42

Answer: 58p   **or**   £0.58

NEVER put both £ and p symbols in your answer.

Mum is cutting a piece of ribbon into equal lengths. The ribbon is 2.1 metres long. How many lengths of 7 cm can she cut?

Tip

If you are using a calculator check the answer in your head by approximating (working out a rough answer).

Solving number problems (4)

Remainders

When dividing, watch out for remainders.

Numbers are not always exactly divisible by other numbers without leaving a remainder.

> 11 is not exactly divisible by 5.
> $11 \div 5 = 2$ remainder 1.

- All odd numbers will have a remainder of 1 when divided by 2.
- All whole numbers are exactly divisible by 1.
- All even numbers are exactly divisible by 2.
- All whole numbers that end in a 0 are exactly divisible by 10.
- All whole numbers that end in 0 or 5 are exactly divisible by 5.

Learn to recognise when a number is exactly divisible by 2, 5, or 10.

Think what a remainder means

When solving a problem and an answer has a remainder, make sure your answer makes sense! Look at this example.

> 25 children are going on a trip. 4 children will fit into each car. How many cars are needed?

$25 \div 4 = 6$ remainder 1

If only 6 cars were taken, 24 children could go and 1 would be left behind!

An extra car is needed so that all 25 children can go!

Answer = 7 cars

Question

42 children are going on a trip. With 4 children in each car, how many cars will be needed this time?

Tip

When dividing and getting a remainder, remember to think about what this remainder means. Check that your answer makes sense.

5 Number patterns (1)

Explaining and continuing a number pattern

If you are asked to explain a number pattern

- be clear.
- find the 'difference' between each number in the sequence by subtracting or by counting on from the smaller number.
- use numbers in your explanation.

Look at this example of a number pattern question:

> Explain and continue this pattern.
>
> 4   11   18   25   32 ....

Now look at this:

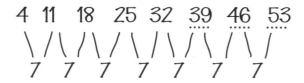

Answer: The numbers in this sequence get larger by a difference of 7 each time.

Sometimes two patterns are combined in co-ordinates. When explaining these, describe the pattern in the first numbers (the **x** co-ordinates) and then describe the pattern in the second numbers (the **y** co-ordinates).

Look at this example: (2, 1) (4, 2) (6, 3) (8, 4) ...

The **x** co-ordinate increases by 2 each time.

The **y** co-ordinate increases by 1 each time.

Tip

Always use numbers in your written answers. Answers like 'Because I guessed' or 'It goes up each time' do not score you any marks!

6 Number patterns (2)

Square numbers

Sometimes, in number patterns, the 'difference' between numbers next to each other is the same.

For example, on page 8 you saw that the difference in the sequence   4, 11, 18, 25, 32 ... is always 7.

In some patterns, however, the difference itself changes, like this:

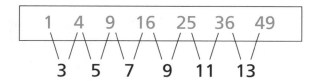

The numbers in the sequence are called square numbers.

Can you see why?

Square numbers are created by **squaring** a number.
A number **squared** means a number multiplied by itself, and 2 squared, for example, is written: 2^2.

1^2 (1 squared) = 1×1 = 1
2^2 (2 squared) = 2×2 = 4
3^2 (3 squared) = 3×3 = 9   These are **square numbers**
4^2 (4 squared) = 4×4 = 16

Example: 5^2 (5 squared) = 5×5 = 25

Question

Answer these in your head:

5 squared =

6×6 =

3^2 =

Activity

On a piece of paper, write down all the square numbers between 0 and 100.

9

7 Fractions

Fractions have a number on the top called the **numerator** and a number on the bottom called the **denominator**.

Look at the fraction $\frac{3}{8}$ ← **numerator**
← **denominator**

The denominator 8 shows the whole has been split into 8 equal pieces.

The numerator 3 shows we are talking about 3 of these pieces. →

Fractions can be **equivalent**. That means they stand for the same amount. To find out if fractions are equivalent, see if there is a pattern in the numerators and denominators.

Fractions like $\frac{1}{2}$, $\frac{2}{4}$ and $\frac{4}{8}$ of a whole are **equivalent**.

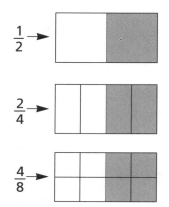

Notice that the **denominator** in each of these fractions is twice as large as the **numerator**.

Question

These fractions are equivalent. Can you say why?

$\frac{1}{3}$, $\frac{2}{6}$, $\frac{3}{9}$, $\frac{5}{15}$

Tip

A quarter is half of a half.

Three quarters of a number can be found by finding a quarter and then multiplying by 3.

8 Decimals

Decimals are numbers that have a **decimal point** to separate the whole numbers (on the left of the dot) from the part numbers (on the right of the dot).

In the number 452.83 there are

452 whole ones, 8 tenths and 3 hundredths.

H T U t h
452.83

Whole numbers . Part numbers

The number of **tenths** is shown in the column to the right of the decimal point.

The number of **hundredths** is shown in the column to the right of the tenths column.

The fraction of this shape that is shaded is $\frac{1}{2}$ or $\frac{5}{10}$.

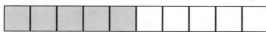

This is 0.5 as a decimal (no whole ones and five tenths).

The fraction of this shape that is shaded is $\frac{3}{100}$.

This is 0.03 as a decimal (three hundredths).

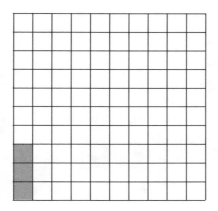

Activity

Learn these:

$\frac{1}{2} = 0.5$ $\frac{1}{4} = 0.25$

$\frac{3}{4} = 0.75$ $\frac{1}{10} = 0.1$

$\frac{2}{10} = 0.2$ $\frac{1}{100} = 0.01$

$\frac{37}{100} = 0.37$

Question

Write $\frac{68}{100}$ as a decimal.

Tip

Ten hundredths is the same as one tenth.
So 31 hundredths is the same as 3 tenths and 1 hundredth (0.31).

9 Percentages

Parts of a whole can be described using percentages too. A percentage is an amount out of 100 and is written like this: **%**.

100% means all of the whole.

50% means half of the whole.

25% means 1 quarter of the whole.

75% means 3 quarters of the whole.

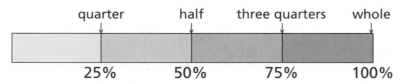

quarter	half	three quarters	whole
25%	50%	75%	100%

10% means 1 tenth of the whole.

40% means 4 tenths of the whole.

1% means 1 hundredth of the whole.

7% means 7 hundredths of the whole.

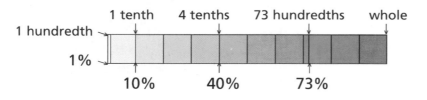

Question

Join the fractions and percentages that stand for the same amount:

$\frac{1}{2}$	75%
$\frac{1}{10}$	37%
$\frac{37}{100}$	25%
$\frac{3}{4}$	30%
$\frac{1}{4}$	50%
$\frac{3}{10}$	1%
$\frac{1}{100}$	10%

Activity

Look out for percentages in shop sales and in magazines. Practise working out how much money you would save if there was 50% or 25% off items.

Tip

Watch out! The same question can be asked in three ways. For example: What is a quarter of 88? What is 25% of 88? or What is 88 x 0.25?

12

10 Negative numbers

Temperature scale

Negative numbers are numbers which are 'on the other side of zero'.

They have a negative sign in front of them, like -6 (minus 6) and -3 (minus 3) to show how many less than 0 they are.

-8 -7 -6 -5 -4 -3 -2 -1 0 1 2 3 4 5 6 7 8

We can see negative numbers on a thermometer.

If the temperature falls beneath 0°C (zero degrees Celsius) we use negative numbers to say how far below zero it has fallen.

The temperature -6°C is colder than -3°C as it is 3 less than -3.

We also say that the number -6 is smaller than -3.

If the temperature was 3°C and fell by 5°C, what would the new temperature be?

Count backwards 5 steps from 3°C to find the answer: -2°C.

Question

Work out the new temperatures:

1 It was -4°C and rose by 8°C.

2 It was 2°C and fell by 7°C.

3 It was -3°C and fell by 4°C.

Tip

When finding temperatures involving negative numbers it helps to draw a quick number line.

TEST YOURSELF

11 Test 1

1. Work these out in your head:

   a. 18 plus 29 ....

   b. 8 multiplied by 6 ....

   c. The sum of 26 and 32 ....

   d. 600 minus 270 ....

   e. Divide 670 by 10 ....

   f. The product of 25 and 8 ....

   g. What is the remainder if 87 is divided by 5? ....

   h. What is 30 cm less than 5 m? ....

2. Work these out on paper:

   a. Calculate 374 + 187 = ...

   b. £3 minus 37p = ...

   c. How many years ago was 1852? ....

   d. Find the total of 75p, £1.50 and £7.75 ....

   e. A journey is 57 km. I have travelled 18 km. How far is there to go? ....

   f. 23 × 6 = ...

   g. 542 multiplied by 5 = ...

   h. 87 ÷ 3 = ...

   i. 872 divided by 6 = ...

   j. If 728 x 63 = 45864, write down the answer to 727 × 63 ....

3. Use a calculator for these:

    a. 58 children are going by car on a trip. Four children can go in each car. How many cars are needed? ....

    b. How many 18 cm lengths of string can be cut from a length of 4 metres? ....

4. Continue and explain these sequences:

    a. 2, 4, 6, 8, ...

    ....

    b. 21, 18, 15, 12, ...

    ....

    c. 1, 4, 9, 16, ...

    ....

5. Work these out in your head. What is …

    a. $\frac{1}{2}$ of 48? ....   **g.** $\frac{1}{2}$ of 15? ....

    b. $\frac{1}{4}$ of 84? ....   **h.** $\frac{1}{4}$ of 68? ....

    c. $\frac{1}{4}$ of 22? ....   **i.** $\frac{3}{4}$ of 100? ....

    d. 0.5 x 20? ....   **j.** 0.25 x 40? ....

    e. 0.75 x 100? ....   **k.** 50% of 90? ....

    f. 75% of 88? ....   **l.** 10% of 800? ....

6. Put a circle around any of these fractions that are equivalent to a quarter.

    $\frac{3}{4}$ $\frac{3}{10}$ $\frac{2}{8}$ $\frac{3}{2}$ $\frac{4}{1}$ $\frac{3}{12}$ $\frac{4}{16}$

7. Write these decimals in order of size, smallest first.

    0.2   0.3   0.22   0.02   2.02   2.0   21.2   20.3

    ....

12 2D shapes (1)

2D shapes are flat shapes that can be drawn on paper. They have no depth.

Names of shapes

triangle 3 straight sides

There are different types of triangle.

equilateral – all the sides are of equal length and all the angles are equal

isosceles – 2 of the sides are of equal length and 2 of the angles are equal

scalene – none of the sides are of equal length and none of the angles are equal

quadrilateral 4 straight sides

Squares, rectangles, parallelograms, trapeziums, kites and rhombi are all quadrilaterals. They all have 4 straight sides.

pentagon 5 straight sides

hexagon 6 straight sides

octagon 8 straight sides

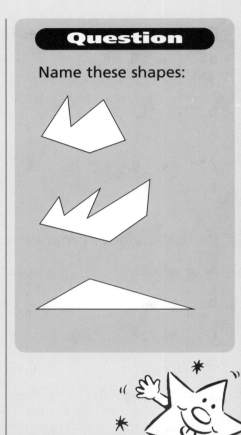

Question

Name these shapes:

Tip

Don't forget that **all** 2D shapes can be regular or irregular! Some people might think that this is not a pentagon! It is!

13 2D shapes (2)

Regular, irregular and congruent shapes

All 2D shapes are either regular or irregular.

A regular shape is one with all its sides the same length and all the angles the same size, like these:

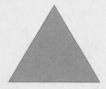

regular triangle
(equilateral triangle)

regular quadrilateral
(square!)

regular pentagon

regular hexagon

regular octagon

Shapes are **congruent** if they are identical in size and shape. They can be turned around or over, but must be the same size and have the same angles.

Other words you might meet:

heptagon
7 straight
sides

nonagon
9 straight sides
sides

decagon
10 straight
sides

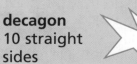

dodecagon
12 straight
sides

Question

Three of these shapes are congruent. Use tracing paper to find the odd one out.

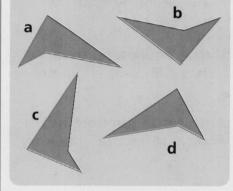

Activity

Look at patterns on wallpaper, curtains and carpets. Are any of the shapes congruent?

Tip

Learn to recognise **regular** shapes because all other shapes are **irregular!**

Reflective and rotational symmetry

A shape has reflective symmetry when it has one or more lines of symmetry (mirror lines).

The first two shapes here have reflective symmetry:

a This rectangle has 2 lines of symmetry.

b This equilateral triangle has 3 lines of symmetry.

c This octagon does not have reflective symmetry.

A shape has rotational symmetry when it will fit into its outline in more than one way, as it is turned (rotated).

If it fits into its outline in 2 ways, we say it has an order of rotational symmetry of 2.

Look at these shapes:

a

b

a has an order of rotational symmetry of 4. It fits into its outline in 4 ways.

b fits into its outline in only one way (order of 1), so this shape does not have rotational symmetry.

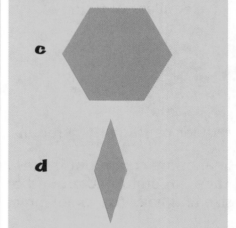

Activity

Find the order of rotational symmetry of **c** and **d**. Use tracing paper to trace the shape. Mark one of the corners, and turn the tracing paper around. Will it fit into its outline in more than one way?

c

d

Tip

When finding lines of reflective symmetry look for all the mirror lines, not just one.

Rotation and reflection

15

Reflecting a shape

Tracing paper is useful when reflecting a 2D shape.

In Diagram 1 the reflected shape B (the image) has the same sized sides and angles as the original shape A, but as a mirror image. Likewise, the reflected shape D is a mirror image of shape C.

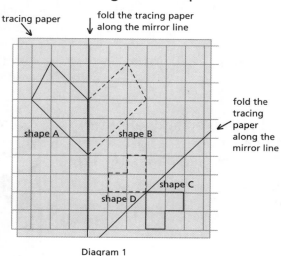

Diagram 1

Rotating a shape

Use tracing paper to rotate a shape through 90° or 180°.

In Diagram 2, shape X is being rotated about point P through 2 right angles (180°). It can be rotated clockwise or anticlockwise.

Notice that the rotated shape Y has the same sized sides and angles as the original shape X, but turned around. Shapes X and Y are congruent.

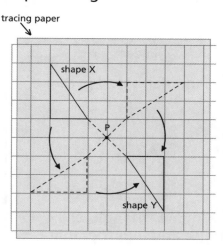

Diagram 2

Question

Use tracing paper to rotate this shape about point P through 180°.

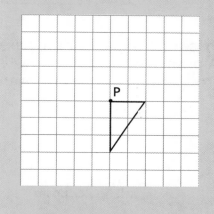

Tip

Remember: you **fold** the tracing paper when reflecting and you **turn/twist** the tracing paper when rotating!

16 3D shapes

3D shapes are solid shapes that have height and width and length.

Cube

Cuboid (rectangular prism)
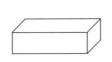

Cone

Prism (triangular prism, hexagonal prism, octagonal prism)
A prism has the same cross-section all along its length. The cross-section can be any of the 2D shapes (see pages 16, 17).

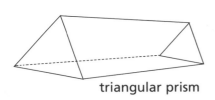

triangular prism

hexagonal prism

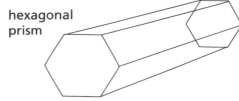

Cylinder (can also be called a circular prism)

cylinder

Pyramid (square-based pyramid, triangular-based pyramid, hexagonal-based pyramid)

square-based   triangular based   hexagonal-based

A pyramid has a 2D base, such as a square, triangle or hexagon. The other faces are triangles and join together at a point.

Nets of 3D shapes

A net is a flat shape or shapes joined together that will fold up to make a 3D shape. You need to be able to recognise these nets which fold to make 3D shapes. (There are more nets which fold to make a square-based pyramid.)

Cube 6 squares

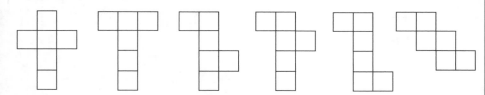

Triangular prism 3 rectangles 2 triangles

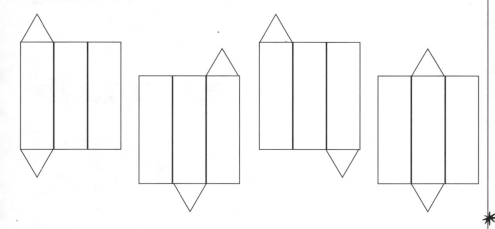

Square-based pyramid 1 square 4 triangles

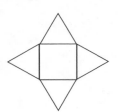 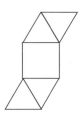

Question

Will net **a** fold to make a square-based pyramid? Will net **b** fold to make a cube?

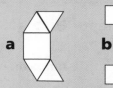

a   b

Activity

Find some empty boxes and carefully open them out flat. Look at the nets. Can you find a box that is a triangular prism or a pyramid?

Tip

Check all the nets in a question carefully. There may be more than one which will make the shape described.

18 Measuring (1)

Units and instruments

When measuring, you need to be able to say:

- what units are used.
- what instruments we use to measure these things.

Measurement	Units (metric)	Instruments
Length height, width, depth, perimeter, distance	**mm, cm, m, km** (millimetres, centimetres, metres, kilometres)	ruler, tape measure, trundle wheel, metre stick
Time	seconds, minutes, hours, days, weeks	watch, clock, timer, stopwatch
Capacity	**ml, l** (millilitres, litres)	measuring jug, cylinder
Mass (weight)	**g, kg** (grams, kilograms)	balance, kitchen and bathroom scales
Angle	° (degrees)	protractor/ angle measurer

You may have learnt the word **weight** instead of **mass** up until now. The correct word to use is **mass** which we measure in kg and g.

Question

Which of these quantities shows the capacity of a cup?

300 kg   300 cm

300 ml   300°

Activity

Use some scales, rulers and measuring jugs to practise measuring.

19 Measuring (2)

Converting from one unit to another

It is important to know how many of one unit make up another, for example, 100 centimetres make 1 metre.

Length: 10 mm = 1 cm   100 cm = 1m   1000 m = 1km

Time: 60 seconds = 1 minute   60 minutes = 1 hour

24 hours = 1 day   7 days = 1 week

$52\frac{1}{4}$ weeks = 1 year   365 or 366 days = 1 year

10 years = 1 decade   100 years = 1 century

Capacity: 1000 ml = 1 l (1 litre)

Mass: 1000 g = 1 kg

Angle: 90° in a right angle   180° in a half turn

270° in $\frac{3}{4}$ of a turn   360° in a complete turn

Activity

On a piece of paper write down your estimates for

• the weight of an apple
• the height of a door
• the capacity of a bucket.

Use measuring instruments to check your answers.

Tip

Have an idea in your head of the size of the units. If you are not sure of one, find out!

Question

Work out these measurements:

half a metre = _____ cm

a quarter of a metre = _____ cm

half a litre = _____ ml

a quarter of a litre = _____ ml

half a minute = _____ seconds

a quarter of a minute = _____ seconds

20 Perimeter, area and volume

Perimeter

Perimeter is the distance around the outside of a 2D shape.
Unit: centimetres (cm) or metres (m).

- Imagine a snail is slithering around this shape.
- How far will it have to go to get back to where it started?
- Draw a trail around the shape, counting as you go.

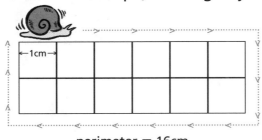

perimeter = 16cm

Area

Area is the amount of space inside a 2D shape.
Unit: centimetre squares (cm^2) or metre squares (m^2)

- Count the squares inside the shape carefully. Watch out for halves or quarters of squares!

Area = $6\frac{1}{2}$ cm^2

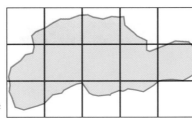

Shaded area = about 8 cm^2

Volume

Volume is the space inside a 3D shape.
Unit: centimetre cubes (cm^3).

- Count the cubes in one layer.
- Count the layers.
- Multiply the number of cubes in one layer by the number of layers.

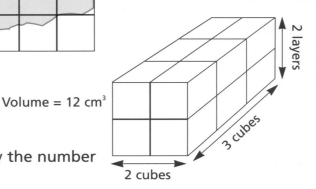

Volume = 12 cm^3

2 layers

3 cubes

2 cubes

21 Reading scales

The key to reading scales on measuring instruments is to look carefully at the numbers on the scale and to follow these steps:

- Pick two adjacent (next door) numbers and find the difference between them.
- Count how many small intervals (spaces) there are between these numbers.
- Work out, by dividing, how much each of these intervals is worth.

For example:

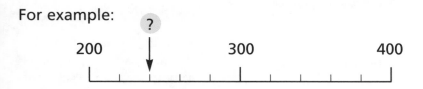

- Two adjacent numbers are 200 and 300. Difference = 100.
- There are 5 intervals (spaces) between them.
- 100 ÷ 5 = 20

Each interval is worth 20, so the arrow is pointing to **240** (200 + 20 + 20).

Tip

When counting intervals, be careful to count the spaces and not the marks on the line. To help you, write any numbers you work out onto the scale

Question

Read these scales. Don't forget to write which units the measurements are (whether they are cm, m, kg, ml, etc.)!

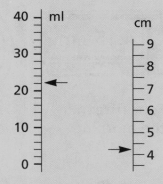

a   b

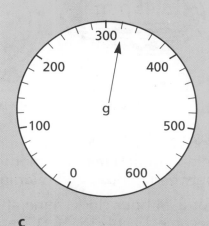

c

Telling the time and 24 hour clock

There are two types of clock: **digital** (the time in figures) and **analogue** (circular clock face with hands).

Digital clocks can be 12 hour or 24 hour clocks.

12 hour digital	**Analogue clock face**	**24 hour digital**

Four fifteen in the morning

Quarter past four

'0' four fifteen

Three forty-five in the afternoon

Quarter to four

Fifteen forty-five

For 12 hour clocks we use **a.m.** to show times between midnight and midday (morning) and **p.m.** to show times between midday and midnight (afternoon and evening).

For a 24 hour clock, remember that after midday, the hours become 13, 14, 15, 16, 17, etc., so that 4 p.m. becomes 16:00 and 6.30 p.m. becomes 18:30.

Adding and subtracting time

You need to be able to work out how long a programme or event lasts or when it started or finished. Remember, there are only 60 minutes in each hour. Ten minutes after 6.55 is not 6.65! It is 7.05.

Add or subtract the whole hours first and then count on, or count back, the extra minutes.

> If a film starts at 11.40 p.m. and goes on for 2 hours 25 minutes, what time does it end?

- **Add the whole hours first and then count on the extra minutes.**

  11:40 p.m. + 2 hours ⟹ 1:40 a.m.
  then count on 25 mins ⟹ 2:05 a.m.

> If a show lasts for 1 hour and 30 minutes and ends at 6.10 p.m., what time did it start?

- **Subtract the whole hours first and then count back the extra minutes.**

  6:10 p.m. − 1 hour ⟹ 5:10 p.m.
  then count back 30 mins ⟹ 4:40 p.m.

Tip

If you are asked to work out what time a T.V. programme starts or ends watch out for a.m. and p.m.

Question

Read this film advertisement. What time will the film end?

The Treasure Cave
$2\frac{1}{2}$ hours of family entertainment
showing at 2.35 p.m.

Activity

Work out how long your favourite TV programmes last, using TV listings in a magazine or newspaper.

The 24 hour clock is often used in timetables.
To read a timetable look across a row and down a column to where these meet.

For example: **Catwoman** is on at the The Point at 18.50.
Batman is on at the ACD Complex at 22.20.

	ACD Complex	Multiscreen	UBI	The Point
Superman	15.20	16.45	18.50	14.30
Catwoman	18.50	19.40	20.40	18.50
Spiderman	20.30	21.45	21.30	20.20
Batman	22.20	23.20	23.15	22.45

If a train travels the same route many times a day this information can be shown in a timetable:

East Grinstead	05:30	06:45	09:00	11:30
Oxted	05:45	07:00	09:15	11.45
East Croydon	06:15	07:30	09:45	12:15
London	07:00	08:15	10:30	13:00
East Grinstead	12:45	13:15	15:00	17:15
Oxted	13:00	13:30	15:15	17:30
East Croydon	13:30	14:00	15:45	18:00
London	14:15	14:45	16:30	18:45

Sometimes the information is shown in two blocks, with the afternoon times below the morning times, as on this timetable.

Question

Look at the train timetable. Which train would you catch to be in London:

by 10.30 a.m.?

by 1 p.m.?

by 17:00?

Activity

Find some timetables in newspapers or magazines. Can you work out what they are showing?

25 Co-ordinates

Co-ordinates tell us where on a grid a point or shape is. Co-ordinates are two numbers inside brackets, with a comma in between, like this (3, 2).

- The first number (the *x* co-ordinate) shows how many places across to move.

- The second number (the *y* co-ordinate) shows how many places up to move.

So (3, 2) means 3 across and 2 up. Use the numbers on the axes to help you plot coordinates.

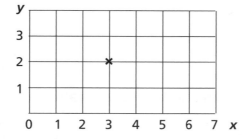

Sometimes you might join points together using straight lines to make a shape, like this:

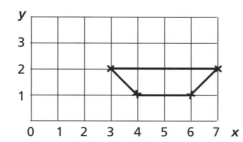

Question

Work out the co-ordinates of the trapezium above.

(,) (,) (,) (,)

Test 2

You need squared paper for question 7.

1. Name these shapes and say whether they are regular or irregular:

A   C   E   G

....

....

B    D   F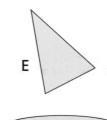

....

....

2. Look at the shapes A, B, C, D above and complete the table:

shape	number of lines of reflective symmetry	order of rotational symmetry
A		
B		
C		
D		

3. Join any congruent shapes.

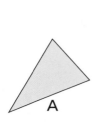 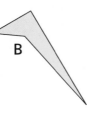 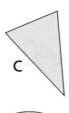  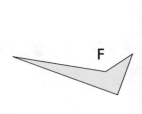

4. What units would you use for...

   a. capacity? ....
   c. mass? ....
   b. time? ....
   d. angle? ....

5. How many...

   a. cm in a m? ....
   b. g in a kg? ....
   c. mm in a cm? ....
   d. m in a km? ....
   e. ml in a l? ....
   f. m in $\frac{1}{2}$ km? ....
   g. minutes in one hour? ....
   h. minutes in 2 hours? ....
   i. g in $\frac{1}{2}$ kg? ....
   j. ml in a quarter of a litre? ....

6. Write these times as a 24 hour clock.

   a. 4 p.m. ☐
   b. 6.30 a.m. ☐

   c. 1.15 p.m. ☐
   d. 3.20 a.m. ☐

   e. 3.20 p.m. ☐
   f. 11.35 p.m. ☐

7. On squared paper, draw a co-ordinate grid and mark these co-ordinates on it. Join them up. What have you drawn?

(8, 9) (6, 9) (5, 8) (5, 6) (4, 6) (4, 8) (2, 8) (2, 6) (1, 6)
(1, 9) (0, 8) (0, 9) (1, 10) (5, 10) (7, 12) (7, 11) (8, 10) (8, 9)

27 Frequency, tallying and bar graphs

A frequency table shows us how many things we have or how often something happens.

To record data quickly we use tallying (lines grouped in fives).

The total (or frequency) is then written into the right-hand column.

These tables are sometimes called tally charts.

Activity

Make a frequency table of traffic passing your house or the end of your road.

Tip

Always give your graph a title, and label each axis. Count tallies carefully and check your answers.

A frequency table showing how many vehicles passed our school in 10 minutes.

Vehicles	Tally	Frequency
Car	ЖЖ ЖЖ I	11
Bus	IIII	4
Lorry	II	2
Other	ЖЖ I	6

We can show this information on a bar graph (or block graph).

A bar graph showing how many vehicles passed our school in 10 minutes.

Frequency

Bars are used to show how many of each vehicle passed the school.

Car   Bus   Lorry   Other

Vehicles

28 Bar graphs and bar line graphs

- Always look closely at the scale (the numbers up the side). These do not always go up in ones.

- Sometimes bars on graphs are drawn as lines. These graphs are called bar line graphs. They can show the same information.

- Bar line graphs are sometimes drawn with the lines going horizontally (across).

A bar graph showing shoe sizes of people in the street.

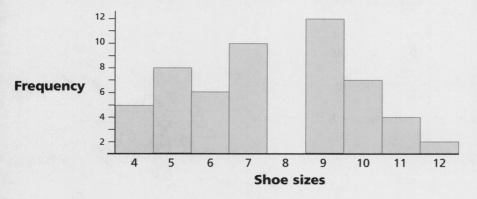

A bar line graph showing shoe sizes of people in the street.

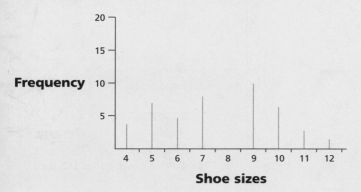

Question

The two graphs on this page show the same information. On one the scale goes up in twos and on the other it goes up in fives. Draw the missing bar on each graph to show 11 people with size 8 feet.

Activity

Make up your own survey and draw a graph. You could ask your friends and family about their favourite foods or TV programmes.

29 Line graphs

Line graphs are another way of showing information. They usually show what is happening during a particular period of time.

Time is shown along the bottom of the graph. Information is plotted and the points are joined together to make a line.

Here is some information about a helicopter's flight during an afternoon.

Time (p.m.)	12.00	12.30	1.00	1.30	2.00	2.30	3.00	3.30	4.00	4.30	5.00
Helicopter's height off ground in metres	0	200	250	250	50	0	0	50	100	100	0

A line graph to show a helicopter's height above the ground, during an afternoon.

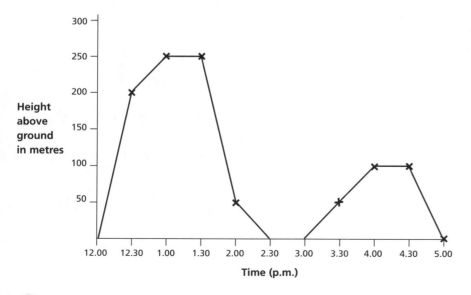

Question

Describe what the helicopter did during the afternoon.

Tip

When answering questions about line graphs, read the title and labels carefully.

Mode, median, mean, range

These are the ages of children in a club:

age	frequency
9	2
10	6
11	1
12	2
13	4

Mode
The mode (or modal value) is the result that occurs most often. In the table above the mode is 10.

Median
When the data is put in order of size, the median is the middle number. Count in from both ends to find the middle.

9   9   10   10   10   10   10   10   11   12   12   13   13   13   13

The middle number is 10, so the median value is 10.

Mean
To find the mean, add the set of values (ages) together.

9 + 9 + 10 + 10 + 10 + 10 + 10 + 10 + 11 + 12 + 12 + 13 + 13 + 13 + 13 = 165

Now divide by the total number of values (children).

165 ÷ 15 (children) = 11   The mean value is 11.

Range
The range is the difference between the highest and the lowest values. In the club the youngest person is 9 and the oldest 13, so the range is 13 − 9 = 4.

Question
What is the mode, median, mean and range of this set of values?

7, 6, 1, 10, 1

Tip
On a simple bar graph the mode is often easy to see. It is the item with the tallest bar!

31 Probability (1)

Words to describe probability

The **probability** of something happening is how **likely** it is to happen.

impossible   unlikely   even or equal chance   likely   certain

- **Impossible** things can never happen: your dog wil never turn into a cat.

- If there is more chance of something not happening than happening, we say it is **unlikely**, like winning the lottery, or rolling a 6 on a dice.

- We say there is an **even** or **equal chance** of something happening when there is the same chance of it happening as not happening, like a coin landing on heads or tails.

Activity

Practise describing the probability of things happening, such as 'It will rain today.' (Likely? Unlikely?) or 'I will watch TV this week.' (Certain? Likely?)

- If there is more chance of something happening, than not happening, we say it is **likely**, like your teacher telling someone off this year!

- **Certain** things will definitely happen, like Tuesday following Monday.

Think about this:

What is the probability (chance) of rolling a 4 on a dice?

Firstly think of all the possible outcomes: 1, 2, 3, 4, 5, 6,

Rolling a 4 is only **1** out of those **6** chances, so we say it is unlikely.

If there is a **1 out of 6 chance**, we can write this as $\frac{1}{6}$.

Tip

Remember that probabilities of real-life things may change each day.

Probability scale

We can use numbers to describe probability. These can be shown on a probability scale, with numbers from 0 to 1.

What is the probability of a coin landing on heads?

Possible outcomes: (1) heads (2) tails

Landing on heads is only 1 out of 2 chances, so has a probability of $\frac{1}{2}$.

We can mark this half way along the probability scale:

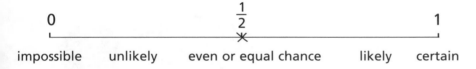

0	$\frac{1}{2}$	1
impossible unlikely	even or equal chance	likely certain

Rolling a 3 on a dice has a probability of $\frac{1}{6}$.

To mark $\frac{1}{6}$ on the scale, we divide the scale into 6 equal pieces, like this:

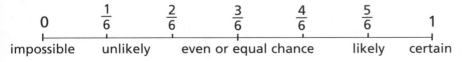

0   $\frac{1}{6}$ $\frac{2}{6}$ $\frac{3}{6}$ $\frac{4}{6}$ $\frac{5}{6}$ 1

impossible   unlikely   even or equal chance   likely   certain

Question

Look at this spinner. Sarah thinks there is the same chance of spinning an even number as spinning a number smaller than 4.

Explain why she is wrong.

Tip

When answering probability questions, always try to include numbers in your answers.

33 Test

1. Complete the end column of this frequency table.

Vehicles	Tally	Frequency
Robin	IIII	
Sparrow	ЖII I	
Blue tit	ЖII II	
Other	I	

A frequency table showing the birds seen on the playground in 10 minutes.

2. Draw the information above onto this bar graph.

Robin   Sparrow   Blue tit   Other

3. Explain what this line graph is showing.

A line graph showing the distance a man travelled from home one morning.

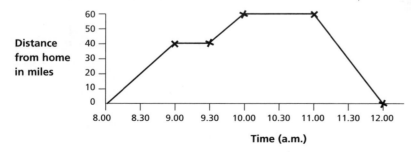

Distance from home in miles

Time (a.m.)

....

....

....

....

4. a. What is the mode, median, mean and range of this set of numbers?

3   4   4   5   5   5   7   8   8   9   12   15   19

Mode .... Median ....

Mean .... Range ....

b. Write a set of three different numbers that have a mean of 9.

....

c. Write a set of five numbers that have a median of 4.

....

d. Write a set of five numbers that have a range of 11.

....

5. a. If an ordinary dice was rolled, draw lines to show how likely these things are:

The number 6 is rolled	Certain
The number 7 is rolled	Likely
A number under 5 is rolled	Even chance
A number under 7 is rolled	Unlikely
An even number is rolled	Impossible

b. Mark the probability that **a number above 4 is rolled** onto this probability scale.

0 ——————————————— $\frac{1}{2}$ ——————————————— 1

34 Algebra (1)

Algebra is where letters such as **a, b,** and **c** are used to stand for numbers. You have to work out what number the letter stands for.

$$3 + a = 5$$

What is on one side of the equals sign has the same value as what is on the other side. So 3 + **a** has the same value as 5. To make the sum balance **a** must be 2.

Look at this:

$$1 + b = 4 + 5$$

What number does **b** stand for?

Thinking of the question as being like a set of balance scales can be helpful!

Add or subtract a number from both sides to leave the letter standing alone on one side.

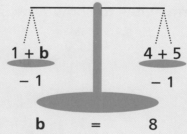

A letter can stand for more than one number.

In a question like $x + y = 10$ whatever **x** stood for would depend on what **y** stood for.

Look at this: $x + y = 10$

If **x** was 0: $0 + y = 10$ so **y** would have to be 10.

If **x** was 1: $1 + y = 10$ so **y** would have to be 9.

If **x** was 2: $2 + y = 10$ so **y** would have to be 8 and so on.

   x could even stand for $\frac{1}{2}$, with **y** as $9\frac{1}{2}$!

Activity

Write on a piece of paper as many different possible answers to **x** + **y** = **10** as you can.

Tip

If you can't 'see' what a letter stands for, think of the balance scales. Add or subtract a number from both sides, leaving the letter alone on one side, and work out your answer!

Algebra (2)

Sometimes letters are used more than once in an equation, like this:

$$a + a + a + a + a = 10$$

To answer this type of question write the equation in a different way.

$a + a + a + a + a$ can be written as $5 \times a$ (5 lots of **a**)

So $\quad a + a + a + a + a = 10 \quad$ becomes $\quad 5 \times a = 10$

5 lots of **something** = 10, so **something** must be 2.

Answer: **a** = 2

Find which number **b** stands for in this equation.

$$b + b + b + b + b + b + b = 21$$

Rewrite this as $7 \times b = 21$

7 lots of **something** = 21, so **something** must be 3.

Answer: **b** = 3

Sometimes, to save even more time, we can write **7b** rather than $7 \times$ **b** or **5a** instead of $5 \times$ **a**, etc.

Question

1. Find which number **r** stands for in this equation

   $r + r + r + r + r + r = 36$

2. Find which number **q** stands for in this equation

   $9 \times q = 90$

Tip

Think of the letter in an equation as being on a flap, with the number it stands for being underneath. When you have 'lifted the flap' (worked out the number) the equation should still work.

36 Angle

An angle is an amount of turn measured in degrees (°).

There are 90° in a right angle and 180° in two right angles (a straight angle).

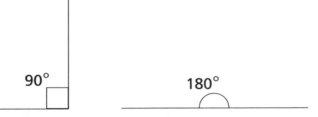

90°   180°

To measure an angle, use a **protractor** or **angle measurer**.

- Line up the centre with the point where the two lines meet.

- Turn the angle measurer until one of the lines is along the zero line.

- Count around from zero, in tens, until you reach the other line.

- Read the scale carefully.

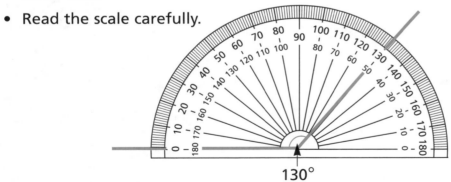

130°

Don't get confused with the two sets of numbers! THINK! Is the angle acute or obtuse? If it is acute, then the angle will be smaller than 90°! If it is obtuse, it will be larger than 90°, but less than 180°!

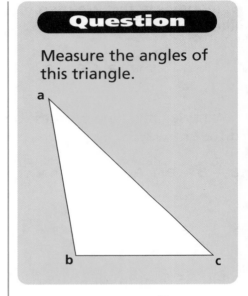
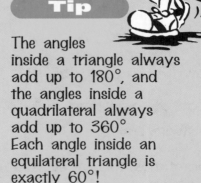

Tip

The angles inside a triangle always add up to 180°, and the angles inside a quadrilateral always add up to 360°. Each angle inside an equilateral triangle is exactly 60°!

42

37 Imperial units

Some years ago Imperial units were used for measuring. Nowadays we use metric units most of the time.

Look at this table:

Measurement	Units (metric)	Units (Imperial)
Length including height, width, depth, perimeter, distance	**mm, cm, m, km** (millimetres, centimetres, metres, kilometres)	inches, feet, yards, miles
Capacity	**ml, l** (millilitres, litres)	pints, quarts gallons
Mass (weight)	**g, kg** (grams, kilograms)	ounces, pounds, stones

Learn to estimate how many of one unit make up another unit.

For example:

2.5 cm is about 1 inch
30 cm is about 1 foot   12 inches = 1 foot
90 cm is about 1 yard   3 feet = 1 yard
1.6 km is about 1 mile   1760 yards = 1 mile

500 ml ($\frac{1}{2}$ a litre) is about 1 pint
1 litre is about 1 quart   2 pints = 1 quart
4 litres is about 1 gallon   8 pints = 4 quarts = 1 gallon

25 g is about 1 ounce
400 g is about 1 pound   16 ounces = 1 pound
6 kg is about 1 stone   14 pounds = 1 stone

Activity

Find rulers, kitchen and bathroom scales and jugs which have Imperial units on them. Try to work out measurements in both metric and Imperial units.

Tip

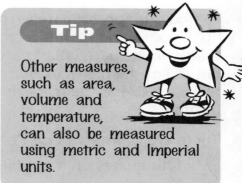

Other measures, such as area, volume and temperature, can also be measured using metric and Imperial units.

38 Pie charts

A pie chart shows information as different sized portions of a circle.

These two pie charts show how two people spend their money.

How Alison spends her money.

How Kevin spends his money.

Alison spends:
- half of her money on food and drink
- about a quarter on clothes
- about one eighth on going to the cinema
- about one eighth on magazines.

Kevin spends:
- two thirds of his money on food and drink
- one quarter on clothes
- only a small amount on magazines
- only a small amount on the cinema.

To find out approximately what fraction of his money Kevin spends on magazines, draw evenly spaced marks around the outside of the pie chart that are the same size as the magazine portion.

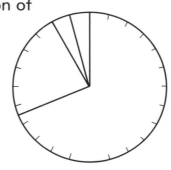

There are 24 intervals, so Kevin spends $\frac{1}{24}$ of his money on magazines.

a
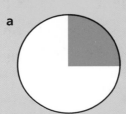

b
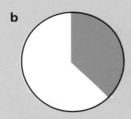

c

d
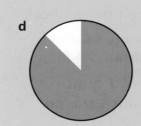

GLOSSARY

acute
(Page 42) an angle that is less than 90°

adjacent
(Page 25) next to

congruent
(Page 19) shapes identical to each other in size and shape are congruent

digit
(Page 4) the 10 symbols we use to write numbers (0, 1, 2, 3, 4, 5, 6, 7, 8, 9)

equation
(Page 41) a mathematical sentence that uses an equals sign. Both sides of the equals sign must balance.

equilateral triangle
(Page 16) a 2D shape which has 3 equal sides and 3 angles of 60°

equivalent
(Page 10) the same value as: 100p is equivalent to £1 and $\frac{1}{5}$ is equivalent to 0.2 and 20%. Fractions are equivalent if they have the same value even though they have different numerators and denominators. These fractions are equivalent $\frac{1}{2} = \frac{2}{4} = \frac{4}{8}$

factor
a whole number that divides exactly into another number. The factors of 18 are 1, 2, 3, 6, 9, and 18.

frequency table
(Page 32) a table showing the number of times something occurs or how many of particular things we have

irregular
(Page 16,17) a 2D shape is

irregular when its sides or angles are not equal

isosceles triangle
(Page 16) a triangle with two sides of equal length and two angles the same size

mass
(Page 22) the amount of matter an object is made from, measured in grams (g) and kilograms (kg).

multiple
a number that is multiplied by another number. Multiples of 3 are 3 (3 × 1), 6 (3 × 2), 9 (3 × 3),12 (3 × 4), etc.

numeral
numerals are symbols we use to write numbers, so 2 and 385 are numerals

obtuse angle
(Page 42) an angle that is greater than 90° but less than 180°

order of rotational symmetry
(Page 18) the number of different ways a shape will fit into its outline when it is turned

parallel
parallel lines stay the same distance apart along their whole length and never meet

prime number
(Page 41) a number that only has two factors, itself and 1. But 1 is not a prime number because it only has one factor

product
(Page 4) the product of two numbers is the answer when we multiply them together. The product of 3 and 4 is 12.

quadrilateral
(Page 16) any 2D shape which has four straight sides. These shapes are all quadrilaterals: square, rectangle, rhombus, trapezium, parallelogram and kite.

reflex angle
an angle that is more than 180° but less than 360°

regular
(Pages 16, 17) a regular 2D shape has all its sides and angles equal

scalene triangle
(Page 16) a triangle which has all its sides of different lengths and all its angles of different sizes

similar
things that have been made larger or smaller but have not changed their shape are known as similar

unit
unit has two meanings in maths:

(Pages 4, 5) (a) In a whole number, the digit on the right is the units digit. This tells us how many ones, or units, we have. In a decimal, it is the digit to the left of the decimal point.

(Page 22) (b) A unit of measurement tells us what we are measuring in, such as metres, grams or millilitres.

ANSWERS

Answers to questions

Page 4
76   120   119   28   39   375   70
600   225   18   13   8

Page 5
927   1679   2710   552   17   8

Page 6
30 lengths

Page 7
11 cars

Page 8
(12, 2) (11, 4) (10, 6) (9, 8)
(8, 10) *x* co-ordinate goes down in
ones, *y* co-ordinate goes up in 2s

Page 9
25   36   9
1, 4, 9, 16, 25, 36, 49, 64, 81, 100

Page 10
You can tell the fractions are
equivalent because in all of them
the denominator is three times the
numerator.

Page 11
0.68

Page 12

$\frac{1}{10} = 10\%$ $\frac{37}{100} = 37\%$

$\frac{3}{4} = 75\%$ $\frac{1}{4} = 25\%$

$\frac{3}{10} = 30\%$

$\frac{1}{100} = 1\%$ $\frac{1}{2} = 50\%$

Page 13
4°C   -5°C   -7°C

Page 16
irregular hexagon, irregular
octagon, scalene triangle

Page 17
b

Page 18
c. order of rotational symmetry of 6
d. order of rotational symmetry of 2

Page 19

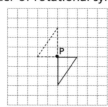

Page 21
a. No; **b**. No;

Page 22
300 ml

Page 23
50 cm   25 cm   500 ml   250 ml
30 seconds   15 seconds

Page 25
a. 22 ml   **b**. 4.5 cm   **c**. 320 g

Page 26
17:00   23:00   20:15

Page 27
5.05 p.m.

Page 28
09:00 from East Grinstead
11:30 from East Grinstead
15:00 from East Grinstead

Page 29
Co-ordinates (3, 2) (7, 2)
(6, 1) (4, 1)

Page 33
A bar line graph showing shoe
sizes of people in the street.

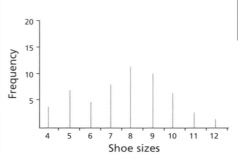

A bar graph showing shoe sizes of people in the street.

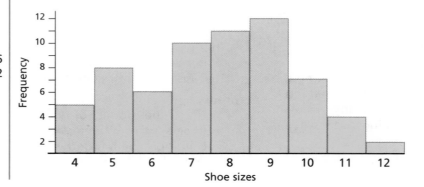

Page 34
Your answer should include this
information: The helicopter takes
off at 12.00. It reaches its highest
point (250 m) at 1 p.m. and stays
there until 1.30 p.m. It lands again
at 2.30 p.m. It takes off again at
3.00 p.m. and lands at 5 p.m. after
flying at 100 m from 4.00 p.m. to
4.30 p.m.

Page 35
mode = 1, median = 6,
mean = 5, range = 9

Page 37
The probability of getting an
even number is $\frac{4}{8}$ and the
probability of getting a number
smaller than 4 is $\frac{3}{8}$. These are not
the same.

Page 41
r = 6; q = 10

Page 42
a. 35°, **b**. 100°, **c**. 45°

Page 44
a. $\frac{1}{4}$, **b**. $\frac{3}{8}$, **c**. $\frac{1}{8}$, **d**. $\frac{7}{8}$

Answers to tests

Test 1   Page 14

1. a. 47   b. 48   c. 58   d. 330
      e. 67   f. 200   g. 2   h. 470 cm
2. a. 561   b. £2.63
      c. 147 (from 1999)   d. £10.00
      e. 39km   f. 138   g. 2710
      h. 29   i. 145 r2   j. 45801
3. a. 15 cars   b. 22 lengths

> If you have given the answers
> 14, 14.5 or 22.2 to the last two
> questions, you are confused over
> the use of remainders in real-life
> contexts. In a real situation 14.5
> cars cannot be driven, or 0.86 of
> a stamp bought, etc. Think how
> to deal with remainders in real
> contexts.

4. a. 10, 12, 14   The numbers
   increase by 2 each time.
   b. 9, 6, 3   The numbers decrease
   by 3 each time.
   c. 25, 36, 49   They are the next
   numbers in the sequence of
   square numbers.
5. a. 24   b. 21   c. 5.5   d. 10
   e. 75   f. 66   g. 7.5   h. 17
   i. 75   j. 10   k. 45   l. 80

> Being able to work out halves
> and quarters of numbers (and
> their percentage and decimal
> equivalents) in your head is very
> important. Work out quarters by
> halving and then halving again.
> Calculating three quarters can be
> done in different ways once one
> quarter is known. If **one** quarter is
> 5 for example, then you can work
> out that three quarters is 15, by
> multiplying by 3: 3 × 15 = 15. Or,
> you can say if one quarter is 5,
> then half is 10, a quarter + a half
> = three quarters: 5 + 10 = 15.

6. $\frac{2}{8}$, $\frac{3}{12}$, $\frac{4}{16}$
7. 0.02, 0.2, 0.22, 0.3, 2.0, 2.02, 20.3, 21.2

Test 2   Page 30

1. a. equilateral triangle – regular
   b. rectangle – irregular
   c. pentagon – irregular
   d. parallelogram (or quadrilateral)
   – irregular
   e. hexagon – regular
   f. octagon – irregular
   g. kite – irregular

> You might think that a rectangle is
> regular, since it is such a familiar
> shape. But the sides are not of
> equal length in this rectangle. The
> only **rectangle** that is **regular** is a
> **square**, since all its sides and
> angles are the same.

2.

Shape	number of lines of reflective symmetry	order of rotational symmetry
A	3	3
B	2	2
C	0	1
D	0	2

> Shapes do not necessarily have the
> same number of lines of symmetry
> as the order of rotational
> symmetry. Always use tracing
> paper to check your ideas.

3. A, C, and E are congruent.
   B and F are congruent.

4. a. millilitres or litres
   b. seconds, minutes, hours, etc.
   c. grams or kilograms
   d. degrees
5. a. 100   b. 1000   c. 10
   d. 1000   e. 1000   f. 500
   g. 60   h. 120   i. 500
   j. 250
6. a. 16.00   b. 06.30   c. 13.15
   d. 03.20   e. 15.20   f. 23.35
7. a dog

Test 3   Page 38

1.

Birds	Tally	Frequency
Robin	IIII	4
Sparrow	IHt I	6
Blue tit	IHt II	7
Other	I	1

2.

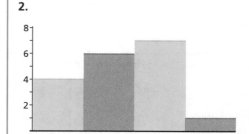

3. A man set off from home at 8.00
   and travelled 40 miles in one hour
   (probably by car). At 9.00 he
   stopped 40 miles from home and
   stayed there for half an hour. At
   9.30 he set off again, travelling
   another 20 miles away from his
   home, in half an hour. At 10.00
   he arrived 60 miles from home,
   where he stayed for one hour,
   until 11.00. It took him one hour
   to travel the 60 miles back to his
   home, arriving at 12.00 noon.

You can also say that he travelled at 40 miles an hour, between 8 and 9 a.m., and between 9.30 and 10, and he travelled 60 miles an hour on his return journey.

4. **a.** mode = 5   median = 7   mean = 8   range =16
   b. any three numbers with a total of 27
   c. any five numbers which, when placed in order of size, have 4 as the middle value
   d. the difference between the largest and smallest number must be 11

5.

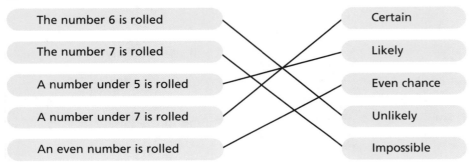

The number 6 is rolled	Certain
The number 7 is rolled	Likely
A number under 5 is rolled	Even chance
A number under 7 is rolled	Unlikely
An even number is rolled	Impossible

6.

0   1